# Ligaments

Naomi D. Karmue

BookLeaf Publishing

India | USA | UK

Made with ❤ on the BookLeaf Publishing Platform

www.bookleafpub.in

www.bookleafpub.com

# Dedication

For my family.
Mommy and Daddy; Anna, Ruth, and Ms.P
You all know all the best and worst parts of me

# Preface

I told myself that I would be a published author before I graduated high school. I am. Only, I saw myself publishing the barely there, three chapter-length novel I have been working on since eighth grade. It is not finished and has undergone yet another rewrite. Not because I lack skill or vision, but because the regard I hold for myself is high; too high. I know perfection eludes us all, but I want to reach it. Even if it is just with the slightest brush of fingertips.

That is what brought me to poetry. It is not perfect. By its own definition it can not be; being a call out of imperfection that it sometimes is. I caught a post on my Instagram about a writing challenge last year. Now, if anyone were to ask, I would tell them that I am a writer. Yes, I write short stories, short blurbs, essays, and have been sitting on several ideas for years. However, I realized the lack of value simply calling myself a writer holds. Anybody could say that they are writers. Owning such a label, being worthy of it, well, that is about quality and having results. So yes. I jumped onto the writing challenge, called my collection *Tissue*, and got my poems published. Now I am a writer, but specifically a poet.

(I would flex but arrogance does not become me.

Even justified.)

Just like that, I had loaded, cocked, and shot; my bullets multiplied like the blue chicks in Angry Birds each landing on their target.

Then I saw another post a year later, and I danced just on the edge for some time. Like a guilty child, I hid myself from my mother until she snuck up on me and pushed me over. Can I admit that that first step–called commitment or whatever– (an old acquaintance, experience of mine) was the easiest part of publishing this second collection? As I truly began writing (which I had done long before, but in this instance) I really understood that just because I liked them did not mean that words liked me. I chose strong emotions as my inspiration for *Tissue*. Afterall, I had the perfect catalyst with the hell that was last year. However, God looked down on me and decided to grant me bliss. I can't write bliss, I swore. Two weeks into the challenge with nothing to show for it I realized how stupid I was:

Would anyone ever choose short chains?
Yes, some people do; but that has never been me. I took hold of my bliss, my ignorance really, and found my muses. A little introspection, a glimpse of my family, my friends, the quiet but expedient ending to this current chapter of my life is coming to, and I found sense. I found words. Words which I put onto the page; edited, revised, force fed to my father and friend, introduced to

my teacher, and created *Tissue*'s younger sister, *Ligaments*. Which I now introduce to you.

Find her sufficient in being because she is love, loss, growth, foolishness, pain. She is family, found and given; she is betrayal and heartache; she is self-confidence, and she is insecurity. She holds everything together while at once breaking it all apart. Discover my *Ligaments*.

# Acknowledgements

First, I want to thank God. Without him where would I be but floating in an abyss surrounded by nothingness as nothingness? I want to thank my family. Mommy, you pushed me to do this, and I am so grateful. And Daddy, you are always my first audience and critic. I would like to thank my English teachers: Mrs. Tack, you have never once dissuaded me out of writing, so I hope these poems are of the utmost quality; and Ms. Lope, for reading and providing feedback on this collection. I am grateful for my friends. Ashley, thanks. You were there for the first one and are still here. Finally, thank you to my inspirations and readers.

# Mouth to Mouth

Freedom tasted like the wind. Her recollection is sweet.
Like the meat in her teeth. Unlike the copper finish of
her face.
A grand sinkhole erupts into a mountain. Continuous
and deep
      in its rise.
And she's stuck. In this sap.
Fading.

Six times. The world has left her and returned.
Color and bleakness blending while she's stuck on the
inside.
Looking out but tethered.
The delicacy of everything escaping her. Here she sits.
Fading.

It so happens, in the glistening of night,
their lives intertwine.

Bright orbs illuminate the massive box she's confined.
Above her, no warmth below, no warmth above her.
She can't help, but to reminisce: her childhood, just
barely begun.
Yet, she's been made new. Destroyed, but

anew.


The sentiment isn't shared.
As she rolls to the edge
Downtrodden, again, that the sky sings on
Downtrodden, because her house is infected
It is hated, but the affection she feels is deep


For him.


Being tarnished by squealers.
She becomes a wave, torrential and wild
Overflowing with everything.
And, at once, soaking through all before her
Stealing breath and crushing beneath her feet.

# Harsh Confessions

I used to be afraid of the dark
He would find me in a dream
he'd chase me through my mind's deepest parts
Where no one could hear my screams

I tried to fight him during the day
but his soldiers were they many
wonders proved did light just lengthen their stay
the battles I lost a plenty

My sisters became cannon fodder
our blanket the hopeless shield
the dark he simply dug in further
My mind for him to yield

Then a harsh twilight found me
weakened, supposedly, with all I could bear
until I watched a man's neck hung from a tree
and recognized the real darkness was there

# Words, When I Need Them

i want to talk about you
but i cannot find the words

*you are the day to my night—*
i begin, and finish

*you are the creature i want to be with always—*
i begin and finish

*you are my person. the one i'll miss most when this is*
*over—*
i begin and finish

*you make me angry—*
i begin and finish

*you are my best–*
i can't say the words together
i look embarrassed
i believe that i am
only of myself

and i look at my mother and her own best—
i don't think i want words

just time that is running away from us
and to take hold of distance
that's what we hide within after all

i want to talk about you, like this
but i cannot find more words
than the words that come to mind

*i'll miss you.*

# With Culture

*Whispered*
I want the fat breast, fat butt look
I want the long fingered french tips
I want the thin neck thin skin attitude
I want those thick thighs and thick lips
I want the big brain energy resting just below
    the big D energy

I'll call it charisma
I'll call it juicy
I'll call it fit
I'll call it polished
I'll call it *gy-at*

I promise, I'll be happy with all of it
Anything that'll make me beautiful
Anything that'll make him see me

# Pretty Little Lying Thing

Oh sweet thing. Should I tell you a secret?

Tears hurt more once they finish falling
They have nowhere to go but into your skin
You hate them for falling; and they know it
They hate you for hating them; so they burn

You try to to dab them away
Preserve yourself
You've done up your face afterall
Tonight, you are a doll

Though the saline has stolen the moisture
That perfect glow you were seeking
All night you have felt like a princess
Suddenly something so small does you in

So cry your heart out; if only to escape the pain
If only to avoid the claw you've allowed into your chest
Do it; feel the mascara run
Forget beauty and think of relief

I promise.
You'll find that and more

In being just mediocre
In the guilt of your tears

# Reflection

I read an old book
and choke on some dust
There I am, or was, really
the illusion of a past
I fully recognize that girl
and I laugh at how
Her idealism sits
on her shoulder
I smile at her words
and balk at the ignorance
She's beautiful, I think
but so young, so stupid
I want to be her again
and I also do not
Because I see her wisdom
so cloaked in hesitance
I look at myself now
a different me
Then there was before
and I am proud
Until I glimpse deeper
into what I will never admit
To storing safely inside
and I realize that I am the same

# Grandpa's Ma

His mother sold us
a known secret they've sown
into hearts of children
a known secret they've threaded
harshly into plump lips

Our silence is a conversation
all punctuation beheaded
Our bodies fill the gaps
all stilted excitement
and our eyes say, "

His mother sold us."

They call us royalty
which is fitting
even with the frigid metal
which weighs us down
heavy as is all expectation

Though we never learn
those practices
Though the grace we have are not
those that they walk with

we are called queens, no miss kings

and our eyes meet with hidden message, "his mother
sold us."

Pretty royal garments are the clothes
brought from back home
Ill-fitting they are, and not
brought for the world
she took us to

And reunions are few and far
with crystal smiles
And overindulges of old customs
with disgrace and disgust and a dissolve way
the torch catchers mumble

For once, out loud, "his mother sold us"

# Signs of the Time

When they say her name I'll faintly hear an echo of her
singing.
I'll look behind me to find her, where she'd often stood,
but she'll be far.
The room we once shared will be slightly bigger, though
all of her clothes
will still be waiting my hands to take. I'll marvel at her
mattress. Slightly
more naked, more desolate, and alone than I—
before deepening an acquaintanceship with my wall.
I'll remember the cold nights I laid beside her warmth
and use it as my
comforter. Though the chill will still eat me up; though
my fear, never
abating alone, is always quick to follow
and I'll tell myself that This is better. This step towards
independence if
only for growth as I remind myself of the harsh late
night lights and
vibrant conversations with a boy I haven't, will never,
meet face to face
that I listened to even as I dreamt.
I'll remember the upset curses that followed me and
haunted me, but were

bitten and scoffed at by me. I'll remember her disorder.
All lasting until I hear a song, catch a show, receive a
gesture.
Then I'll remember my older sister. Her place in my heart
empty now
leaving me an ounce lighter than I should be.
I'll blanch at her departure while offering to take her to
the plane.

# The Little Wants

Teach me how—
Teach me how to *GLOW*
I am but a dim light flickering in the wind

I burn through my wick
and turn my wax to gooey liquid
mush
I just barely catch onto the next candle before I am
forever put out

I sway dangerously from my wire
My bulb doesn't shine
It rejects luminosity.

How will anyone find me in the darkness that I've
become?
How can you?
Is it too late?

Am I
Too dull?

I want to be with the
*STARS*

Teach me how to fly
Let me be with you
Let me soar

Fix my tattered, naive wings
Give them the push they desire
I cannot break gravity on my own
I am lame

Futility smiles behind my eyes
Hatred swells within
I want

# Father Nature

Nature has never belonged to me
As I have never allowed myself
to be owned by him

He sends in recruiting agents:
Wind, Race, Rain, and Gender
They come equipped with their confines
He's taught them the way of persuasion
Though they prefer the debilitation of mind

I call him my foe, but Nature knows that
he cannot touch me
'Cause I see past the illusion that he casts
    and I know
Nature could never hope to contain me

# Delight in Itself

I am irrationally and perpetually sad.
Understand this, foremost,
Whence you can, whisper to me.
Answer this: *aren't you?*

Could my dolor fill Mommy's cast iron?
It could. It could overflow.
Flood the house on Holly tree lane.
continue from there.

It could spread to the downstream streets
carry away the game of Rhodes
to the bowling expanse of azure.
continue from there.

It could fill the far-off particle holes
looming menacingly with their seductive light.
It could cause supernovae; become the blanket of night.
continue from there.

It could.
Profound as it is. It could.
Considerable as it is. It could.
and continue from there.

Yet it won't.
in its everything,
you'll find its containment, within this vessel,
Call it security

For when I ask, *aren't you?*
You whisper to me, understanding on your lips,
you are as I am, yet,
"I feel euphoric"

# Worth Something

Flaps its wings in the rain
Silver lined in the diamond light
Glittering as it soars through a sunless sky
    You like the gray, dull
It allows its wings to catch the wind

Loses itself in the barely there chill
Then falls. Gravity given its chance
It hits the ground.
This black, gold bird.
    You like the dirt brown
Its silver wings broken, tarnished due to

Lies there a pitiful thing
Once golden eyes, what's worse than bronze?
What's worse than copper?
Course
    You like the spreading rust.
It waits; first deaths last

Waits, it supposes
For someone to pick it up
Fix it up
Make it sparkle, fly

You like wretchedness

It wants someone to say that it is something

# The Child Fallacy

It screams out at Its youth.
Too short to get to the top, but unsighted hindsight spurs
It.
So, It jumps. It climbs. It tries, and fails, to fly.
Falling each time. Failing all the others.

It screams out at its youth.
Lies in the shade when It's full, and basks
in the light when hunger becomes excitement.
Yet It tires quickly. Grasping at the day.
(Appalled when it slips from Its fingers)

It screams out at Its youth.
Ascendence traps it like a shadow, as such
    epidermis withers off in even gentle breeze.
At last, a melancholic voice rises.
For the end is the edge of lightness.

# The Underappreciated

Learn me your discipline
That which is etched to my soul
Once your disordered scribbles mar my skin

Begin the marking at my edges
Hold fast to the festering wound
Yank. Until it becomes me

Through you, and only you
I am made ignorant
And in ignorance—my mortality

The vulnerability bleeds as it is wont to
You scavenged, you found
Your own treasure

When my eternity calls forth your disgust
You tremble at it. Your bones quake
It's rational, that you draw up arms

Here I am
Stuttering my steps; thinking
I can still keep you

Before you tremble at my hubris
You attack
And I am the monster

# Libra

Her mother is the sun. She is the planet stuck in her
orbit
Almost, she is, like all of the other rocks, gaseous balls
Only, her matter consumes her from the core.

Life cannot withstand her atmosphere
In turn, she cannot withstand life
There is where anguish lies

She lashes out at the meteors. Fracturing them to pieces
She steals their children to feed on
They give her no nourishment. She grows frail

Like a flame she is alluring and beautiful
She is, as well, volatile and hateful
So spurned is she in her lonely orbit

Born of life and love though finding them not to her
taste
Unwilling to embrace the frigidness or rockiness or
gaseousness of another
She faces billions of miles of a vast space in silence

# Name One Adjective

My running feet don't make noise
They're so quick, you're gonna blink and miss me
Blink and I'm back.
Don't you know,
I'm like Quicksilver speeding into the bullet

My running feet are gonna *carry* me to you
Just whisper a need.
You know that I'll be there and out
just as fast
When need turns to want and want disappears.

# The Size of Awareness

How small this new lump before me
I laugh at its impotence, and exclaim "How small!"
How small! it is than the obstructions preceding
In comparison it is trivial.
Nothing.

Merely a minor hindrance.
It has not the strength to break wind.
Nor does it hold potential.
Yet I stumble before it?
*No.*

Only an opportune loss of footing.
I call to stability
She does not come.
I call on good fortune
She has been spent.

The ground reaches up to me
I laugh at my own impotence.
And the lump near my feet
it exclaims, "How small!"
Such perspective

Comprehension eludes me.
Far too late, I'll scream
with the colossal impact.
Where is wisdom
but within the lump?

# Restless Spirits

Leave peacefully.
my knees chafe and hands have grown stiff
under your gaze,
I abhor the Desparables.
and you—
Here you faze into one of their kind
Stealing and trampling the hearts of my rearers
I recoil at your spew, and
in the same sense
do you see our fortress crumble
or are you satisfied with the scars marking your rampage

Leave peacefully
That your hush,
what will be left,
may echo rather than.
Take your seat at our table
and remove it
remove your cup from our cupboard
for your own relief, and
for ours
Depart not like the wind
though, post haste
and

Leave peacefully
that our hearts retain those shards
not already taken as your captives.

# Choke Cherry

Wow!
Is that dark tree on your back a scar of vines?
Are those bracelets on your wrists jewels unasked for?
Do you quiver from the domineering voice of man
as the voice of man has knocked you down before
unaware; compliant?
Has your sovereignty been stripped
given by you or taken by Emmanuel's thief?
You hear the reverberation once
asphalt rockers, dust turners, grass jumpers
Finding a wand suitable for your cultivation.
See you misplaced in your new nicotine rush
A dead cause reawakened for individual self-importance
Upholding the cataracts
Purging the life the from the Titans
Is it yours to take?

# In Providence

providence is under construction
she gives him her body
lying docile to his digs
whatever he makes her she becomes


she is too willing to become


rural; for him
she catches hanahaki
the vines and flowers
they make her pretty
he says as much
until the trees and bushes hide too much of her


then she becomes


suburban; for him
she embraces mediocrity and conformity
she adopts the weekly trim
she glows in maturity
he tells her
but how can he still have her with her laugh paper thin


so she becomes

urban; for him
she swallows smoke and is noise
she chases the wind and delights in its slip
he likes her wild
he promises
lasting as long as his lungs can

finally she becomes

providence; for her
she blinks off rose tint
the shovel is heavy in her hands
but it is autonomy
that gives her strength

# Glass Relations

Shattered glass chases my heart into a pit.

Genuine crystal—none of the Plexi-glass stuff
but real, hard, fragile silica—is a novelty
     of age

Though the substance, as described, is difficult
     to find, it is the most dreadful of untruths
when one attests to not have search for such
     treasure.

It is a fact, undeniably, where I will meet you and
     you I
even amid whichever storm dividing us,
that our glasses are kept in high cabinets

Those which we stretch and contort to reach
and those which we protect and conceal from
     the adversary glare

Let dust fall on them; do you, like I, not shudder?

Let the smallest of imperfections mar the smooth
     skin; do you, like I, not grow faint?

Maintenance calls us to polish and shine.
We begin with pure cloths, warm water, fragrant
    soap.
Further on, the cloth grows less pure, the water cools.
What's more, fragrance becomes repellent?

Few among us can beat the dust from the cloth,
Fewer more can stand idly over a heating pot
Even less can discover pleasure in annoyance

Yet it does fracture the soul to watch
    cracks crawl slowly over glass

And the pieces sting once they have
    embedded themselves in palms
    in hearts

And the scars heal.

But the glass will never just be glass
Patch works until it does not

www.ingramcontent.com/pod-product-compliance
Lightning Source LLC
LaVergne TN
LVHW010915200726
843509LV00013B/1950